Glossary

of

Computer

Terms

REVISED EDITION

Aman Saikia

64-bit/32-bit: This denotes the number of "pieces" (or bits) of information required by an operating system to run a certain application. Windows XP, Windows Vista and Windows 7 have 32 bit as well as 64 bit versions. More bit means that data can be processed larger chunks and system can address a larger number of locations in physical memory.

A

ACCESS TIME: The length of time required for a binary word in the memory section of a computer to be read by the Central Processing Unit (CPU), or the time to read data from a peripheral data storage area.

ACCUMULATOR: An interface Register (memory) in the Arithmetic Logic
Unit (ALU), which stores interim arithmetic information for future processing.
The accumulator is interface between the ALU and other sections of the computer.

ADDER: The digital logic circuits in the ALU section of a computer which implements the adding process (sum and carry) of two or more binary numbers.

ADWARE: A software program that is designed to run once a web page has been accessed. This is usually in the form of banner or popup advertisements. Adware can also be designed to be installed on your system without your consent or knowledge. These forms of adware are usually referred to as "spyware" and are used to monitor your surfing habits so that their software can deliver better targeted advertisements.

ADDRESS: The location of digital information in the Memory Unit of a computer, or a digital code that designates this location.

ALGORITHM: The sequence of operations that defines a solution to a problem in logic.

ALPHANUMERICS: The term that defines the letters of the alphabet (A to Z)
and the ten numerals (0 to 9). The term is generally used to mean any text data.

AMERICAN STANDARD CODE FOR INFORMATION INTERCHANGE (ASCII): A 7-bit binary code, providing 128 different binary combinations for standard American keyboards. ASCII is used to encode all 26 letters of the alphabet (upper and lower case), all ten decimal digits (0 to 9), punctuation marks, standard graphics, and special control codes into machine language.

Although ASCII has 128 different codes, only 7 bits are needed for each different code. ASCII characters are generally stored inside 8-bit bytes, providing room for the 128 ASCII codes plus another 128 codes, totalling 256 characters. This 8-bit code is referred to as EXTENDED ASCII.

ANSI: It stands for American National Standards Institute. This is the place that sets standards for data communications, like the Internet.

ANALOG: Not digital. This is data in the form of a continuous flow. A record or a tape is analog. Digital, on the other hand, is in pieces or samples.

ANONYMOUS FTP: Using the FTP function of the Internet anonymously by not logging in with an actual, secret login ID and password. Often permitted by large, host computers who are willing to share openly some of the files on their system to outside users who otherwise would not be able to log in. ftp.apple.com and ftp.microsoft.com are two software company sites.

AOL: America On-Line used to be the largest bulletin board system in the world. With the advent of AOL v3.0 though, AOL has become the largest Internet Service Provider in the world. Unfortunately, AOL is available in only large metro areas. It is also the largest provider of blank diskettes in the world.

APPLESHARE: This is Apple Computer's network system. It allows many different end users (people on computers) to attach to one central location and get files.

APPLET: A small Java application that is downloaded by an ActiveX or Java enabled web browser. Once it has been downloaded, the applet will run on the user's computer. Common applets include financial calculators and web drawing programs.

APPLICATION: Computer software that performs a task or set of tasks, such as word processing or drawing. Applications are also referred to as programs. It does things when called upon.

ARITHMETIC LOGIC UNIT (ALU): The section of a computer that contains a large amount of logic circuitry and performs the four basic arithmetic functions (addition, subtraction, multiplication, and division). Larger units contain circuitry for higher mathematical functions, such as: quadratic equations, etc.

ARCHIE: Search tool used to find resources stored on Internet-based FTP servers.
ARTIFICIAL INTELLIGENCE: It is the technique with which a machine is made to think and take decisions like human beings.

ASSEMBLER: A software program that converts (translates) each symbolic instruction written in ASSEMBLY LANGUAGE into the MACHINE LANGUAGE (binary code) of a computer.

ASSEMBLY LANGUAGE: A programming language (source code) that consists of a group of coded letters or labels, called mnemonics. A mnemonic is a memory assist to help recall data. Each mnemonic represents a single instruction that is translated into the binary code of machine language. Mnemonics are easier to use than machine language instructions.

For example, the mnemonic "MUL" tells the computer to "Multiply".

ASYNCHRONOUS: A term that describes a non-clocked, or free-running digital signal that triggers successive computer instructions; the completion of one instruction triggers the next. The speed of operation depends only on the speed of the signal generated through the circuit or network. In contrast with SYNCHRONOUS operation, the computer clock controls the speed of the signals in the system. Transferring data with the help of start and stop bits that indicate the beginning and end of each character being sent.

ASP: Active Server Pages. An invention from Microsoft that runs on their server software.

AVI: Stands for Audio/Video Interleaved. Microsoft's format for encoding video & audio for digital transmission.

B

BACKPLANE: A part of a computer into which the system's PC boards are plugged to provide a common voltage supply, reference, and SYSTEM BUS for all computer sections. A backplane is often called a MOTHERBOARD.

BACKBONE: Well, all of these computers have to come together somewhere.

There are many "backbones" on the Internet. Think of the backbone as the next larger grouping of computers you connect with to get included in the Web. You're at the end of a rib coming off of the backbone—get the picture? The main backbone of the Internet here in the U.S. is the NSFNet. It stands for National Science Foundation Net.

BANDWIDTH: The capacity of a networked connection. Bandwidth determines how much data can be sent along the networked wires. Bandwidth is particularly important for Internet connections, since greater bandwidth also means faster downloads.

BASIC: The acronym for Beginner's All-purpose Symbolic Instruction Code.
BASIC is an easy to use programming language, originally intended for educational purposes; it is available for personal computers in varying degrees of complexity.

BAUD RATE: (i) This is a measurement of the amount of data that can be transferred in one second. (ii) This is an industry-accepted method of measuring modem speed. Baud rate divided by eight equals transmission speed in bytes per second.

BAUDOT CODE: A 5-bit digital code having 32 possible combinations of binary "0" and "1"; for Teletype (Telex) communications systems.

BENCHMARK: The specifications for measuring the characteristics of a computer system, or parts of the system, under clearly-defined conditions.

BIOS: Stands for Basic Input/output System. This is the little set of programs that lets all the different parts of the computer talk to each other.

BINARY CODE: The most basic language a computer understands, it is composed of a series of 0s and 1s. The computer interprets the code to form numbers, letters, punctuation marks, and symbols.

BINARY CODED DECIMAL (BCD): A coding system in which each decimal system numeral (0 to 9) is represented by a 4-digit (4-bit) binary code.

BINARY SYSTEM (BASE 2): A numbering system consisting of only two digits (0 and 1), as contrasted with a DECIMAL SYSTEM that uses ten digits (0 to 9). In electronics, "binary" and "two-state" are synonymous.

BINARY DIGIT (BIT): The term "BIT" is the contraction of Binary Digit and is part of a binary WORD that consists of combinations of "0" and/or "1". There are only two numerals in binary arithmetic (base 2) and is the basis for binary code (Machine Language), the language of the computer. A "bit" has the same significance in binary arithmetic that a decimal digit has in the more familiar decimal (base 10) arithmetic system.

BISTABLE MULTIVIBRATOR: A digital circuit having two stable electrical states. The output signal of this circuit will remain in either state (0 or 1) indefinitely until an external input signal causes the circuit to switch to its other output state. This circuit is generally called a FLIP-FLOP.

BINHEX: Converts a Macintosh program into ASCII text for transmission over the Internet. Files with a .hqx extension are BinHex. Aladdin's Stuffit Expander converts BinHex documents back into their true form.

BLACK BOX: A term that refers to an electronic circuit or system within an enclosure without necessarily providing details of its internal elements. The black box concept often offers a useful approach in the design of a system or in the interconnect between two circuits or systems.

BLOG: (Slang term for a Weblog) A blog is a person journal that can be accessed publicly and allow people to comment on the previously posted comments. When someone posts a comment to a blog this is called "blogging". The person that owns the blog is called a "blogger". Most typically, blogs are updated on a daily basis and use the most basic of formats so that a person with very little background in computing can easily figure out how the blogging system works.

BLU RAY: Also known as Blu-ray Disc. This is an optical disc format that was developed to enable recording, playback, and rewriting of high-definition (HD) video. This technology has a storage capacity far greater than that of traditional DVDs. A single-layer disc can hold up to 25GB while a dual layer disc can hold up to 50GB. DVD disc technologies use a red laser to read and write data. Blu-ray uses a blue-violet laser (hence the name). The benefit of the blue-violet laser over the red laser is its ability to focus the laser spot with greater precision because of its shorter wavelength.

BLUETOOTH: Radio technology that connects electronic devices without using a cable. Data and voice can be exchanged at ranges of up to 10 meters without the need for devices to be lined up together.

BMP: (pronounced "bimp"): It is a Microsoft Windows image file made up of little dots.

BOOLEAN ALGEBRA: Named after George Boole, a 19th century English mathematician, who first formulated theorems that included a mathematical analysis of the laws of human logic. It uses algebraic-like notation to describe the interaction of variables having only two states: "true" and "false". In electronics, the states are often referred to as "1" and "0" or, "high" and "low".

BOOTSTRAP (BOOT): A software program for initiating the operation of a computer. The function of the program is to set up the input and output (I/O) devices and load the OPERATING SYSTEM from a disk, cassette, or built-in READ ONLY MEMORY (ROM).

BOOT: To start up a computer. Cold boot—restarting computer after having turned off the power. Warm boot—restarting computer without having turned off the power.

BREAKPOINT: Location of a place in a program where program execution can be stopped to permit a visual test, printing, or other performance analyses.

BROWSER: User's software program for viewing & browsing information on the Internet. Software that enables users to browse through the cyberspace of the World Wide Web. Netscape Navigator and Microsoft's Internet Explorer are the two primary Web browsers today.

BUBBLE MEMORY: A high-density memory medium upon which a magnetic film is grown on a gadolinium-gallium garnet substrate. A small permanent magnet is mounted inside its package, perpendicular to the surface of the substrate. When an external magnetic field is created with an external coil, magnetic "bubble" domains are formed on the internal magnetic film which represent patterns of "1s". The absence of magnetic bubbles will represent patterns of "0s".

BUFFER: The buffer is a section of the computer where data is stored before being used. This buffering allows time for an application to fix differences in bit rates among other things. It creates a space of time for compensation.

BUNDLED: A term describing a computer system that includes all necessary hardware and software that will allow the system to operate as advertised.

BUS (BUSS): There are wires between all the parts of your computer. There is a wire from the memory to the brain, and from the brain to the printer, etc. Those wires are called busses. They differ from one another by the amount of data they will transfer at one time.

BUS CONTROLLER: A circuit that generates commands and control signals for sequencing and timing of the data transmitted on a bus.

BURST: Most people know this from "pipeline burst cache." Burst means to send data in a large package all at one time rather than small bits over a longer time.

BUG: A malfunction due to an error in the program or a defect in the equipment.

BYTE: A byte is a computer data transfer or data storage measurement. One byte equals 8 bits.

C
C: A programming language developed at AT&T.

CACHE: Web browsers store accessed information in a folder on your hard drive called a cache. Some also store information in memory for faster access. This saves time when a user goes to another page on a site with the same graphics. The Iowa Newspaper Association site uses many of the same graphics throughout to take advantage of this feature to speed browsing.

CAD-CAM: Computer Aided Drawing-Computer Aided Manufacturing. The instructions stored in a computer that will be translated to very precise operating instructions to a robot, such as for assembling cars or Laser cutting signage.

CD-ROM (COMPACT DISK READ-ONLY MEMORY): An aluminized disk, 4.72" in diameter that provides an optical storage medium for digital data up to

650 Megabytes. A laser beam permanently burns data into its surface which cannot be over-written, altered, or erased, providing read-only memory capability. Larger size disks are generally called "laser disks".

CD-R or WORM (COMPACT DISK, WRITE ONCE, READ MANY
MEMORY): A blank disk that can be programmed once, permanently storing up to 650 Megabytes of digital data. Once programmed, it has essentially the same features as a CD-ROM.

CD-E or CD R/W (COMPACT DISK, ERASABLE, READ/WRITE
MEMORY): Capable of storing up to 650 Megabytes of digital data. It uses a magneto-optical technology that combines the storage capacity and reliability of optical disks and the erasability of magnetic media.

CGA: Stands for Color Graphics Adapter. It's a piece of hardware that plays with colours.

CGI: Common Gateway Interface. A programming standard that allows visitors to fill out form fields on a Web page and have that information interact with a database, possibly coming back to the user as another Web page. CGI may also refer to Computer-Generated Imaging, the process in which sophisticated computer programs create still and animated graphics, such as special effects for movies.

CHARACTER GENERATOR: A circuit that accepts digital data and forms the corresponding letters and numerals for a monitor or printer.

CHAT: Typing text into a message box on a screen to engage in dialog with one or more people via the Internet or other network.

CHIP A tiny wafer of silicon containing miniature electric circuits that can store millions of bits of information.

CLIENT/SERVER: Computer technology that separates computers and their users into two categories: clients or servers. When you want information from a computer on the Internet, you are a client. The computer that delivers the information is the server. A server both stores information and makes it available to any authorized client who requests the information.

CLIPBOARD: A temporary data (text and graphics) storage facility used when transferring data to a new location.

CLOCK: A digital pulse generator that controls the timing of a computer and, to a great extent, determines the speed (number of instructions per second) capability of the computer. Generally, it is located in the CPU.

CLONE: An imitation or copy of the original. Usually refers to building a computer system that is based on and compatible with another computer company's system.

CLUSTER: In a Windows environment, Cluster refers to the allocated space within files measured in units. A cluster is part of a group of a logical disk sector. Cluster can also refer to a group of computers networked together and used as a single unit.

CLUSTERING: This is a way of connecting two (or more) computers together using clustering hardware so that they share the processing load. If ten computers of equal processing speed are clustered together, you would in a sense have a single computer with ten times the processing capacity. The most common use of this technique is with search engines where it is used to provide speedy search results. A couple of other common uses of clustering can be to increase storage capacities or for networks that require load balancing to increase a networks availability and stability.

CMOS LOGIC: A CMOS technology monolithic IC "logic family" characterized by low power dissipation per gate, high chip density, and relatively high propagation delay per gate compared with bipolar IC logic families.

COBOL: Stands for Common Business Oriented Language.

CODEC: Short form for Compressor/Decompressor. This technology is used for compressing and decompressing data. Codecs are widely used in both hardware and software. A few examples of codecs are: Cinepak, Indeo and MPEG.

COM: Stands for Component Object Module.

COMPILER: A software program that converts (translates) a complete software program written in high-level language SOURCE CODE (such as PASCAL or FORTRAN) into machine language. The entire source code is edited, compiled, and run at one time as compared to an INTERPRETER that is run one line at a time. This is an application that converts a programming language into a machine language program.

COMPLEMENT: Reversal of bit values: "1s" become "0s" and "0s" become
"1s".

CONCURRENCY: The independent execution of two or more sequences of events that are either occurring, or appearing to occur simultaneously.

CONSOLE: The term referring to a combination of a DISPLAY and
KEYBOARD.

CONTROL BUS: A set of transmission lines whose function is to carry synchronization signals and control data as part of the SYSTEM BUS.

CONTROL UNIT (CU): Part of the CPU containing the CLOCK, PROGRAM
COUNTER and INSTRUCTION REGISTER. The CONTROL UNIT also generates control signals and manages the CONTROL BUS.

COOKIE: A text file sent by a Web server that is stored on the hard drive of a computer and relays back to the Web server things about the user, his or her computer, and/or his or her computer activities.

COUNTER: A circuit whose output(s) change state in a specified sequence on receiving appropriate input signals. The circuit can provide a required output pulse after receiving a specified number of input pulses.

COUNTERFEITING: People make duplicate CDs of original software and sells them at low price.

CPU: Stands for Central Processing Unit. This is the brain of your computer.
It is made up of two parts: The Arithmetic Logic Unit (this does all the processing) and the Control Unit (this makes sure every part of the computer is working together to present the information).

CRACKER: A person who "breaks in" to a computer through a network, without authorization and with mischievous or destructive intent.

CRASH: A hardware or software problem that causes information to be lost or the computer to malfunction. Sometimes a crash can cause permanent damage to a computer.

CSS: Stands for Cascading Style Sheets.

CURSOR: A moving position-indicator displayed on a computer monitor that shows a computer operator where the next action or operation will take place.

CYBERSPACE: This is a term that gives us a way to sort of "see" what we are surfing while on the Net. It's a generic term for the entire Internet, not just the World Wide Web.
2. Slang for the Internet.

D

DAISY-WHEEL PRINTER: An impact printer that uses a print element shaped like a flat disk or large thimble to form the alphanumeric and punctuation marks that are part of its print element. Unlike dot-matrix, ink-jet, and laser printers, daisy-wheel printers cannot print graphics. See LETTERQUALITY
PRINTER.

DATABASE: A collection of similar information stored in a file, such as a database of addresses. This information may be created and stored in a database management system (DBMS).

DATA: Anything that is recorded or used for processing. The stuff that transfers between computers needed a name — data seemed good.

DATA RATE: Speed that information moves from one item to another. This is usually in the form of bits.

DATA-BASE MANAGEMENT SYSTEM (DBMS): A software program that controls and supervises the updating, editing, and execution of items from multiple files in a data base environment.

DDR: Stands for "Double Data Rate." A type of advanced SDRAM designed to deliver data at a double rate of speed for a given clock frequency.

DEBUG: The process of detecting, locating, and correcting a problem in a software program or hardware.

DECODER: A software, hardware or circuit that is designed to translate a coded or scrambled signal in to a readable form. A common use for this is by cable companies that scramble a signal until a subscriber becomes authorized to view the signal. The cable company then decodes the signal in to a viewable form.

DECRYPTION: This is a process of converting information in to a readable form that has been encrypted by the use of an encryption algorithm. A common use could be that a person would like to protect sensitive data that resides on their computer system, so they would use an encryption software to scramble the information. The same software that scrambles the information would be the only authorized entity to decrypt the information. This software could be made available to any authorized person for decryption purposes at other locations.

DECREMENT: The reduction of the numerical contents of a counter. A decrement of 1 is usually assumed, unless otherwise specified. It is the complementary operation of INCREMENT.

DEFAULT: The pre-defined configuration of a system or an application. In most programs, the defaults can be changed to reflect personal preferences.

DESKTOP: The main directory of the user interface. Desktops usually contain icons that represent links to the hard drive, a network (if there is one), and a trash or recycling can for files to be deleted. It can also display icons of frequently used applications, as requested by the user.

DESKTOP PUBLISHING: The production of publication-quality documents using a personal computer in combination with text, graphics, and page layout programs.

DEVICE: In a computer system, this term refers to a unit of processing equipment external to the CPU. It is sometimes synonymous with the term PERIPHERAL.

DEDICATED LINE: This is a phone line meant specifically for one thing, like being attached to a computer.

DEMODULATION: This is the process of converting analog information (like over phone lines) into digital information (like in a computer). See "Modem" for more.

DIAL-UP LINE: This is a telephone line that is connected to a server. When it is called, tones are exchanged between the server and the devise calling in order to attach.

DIAL-IN: An Internet account that can connect any stand-alone computer directly to the Internet. The account is used by having a computer-based software application dial-in to an Internet service provider (ISP). The software connects with the ISP and establishes a TCP/IP link to the Internet that enables your software to access Internet information. The computer that accesses a dial-in connection needs either a modem to connect via a regular phone line or a terminal adapter (TA) to connect via an ISDN phone line.

DIGITAL: Your CD player is digital. It is a series of small samples of data playing together very quickly (30,000 times a second). Digital recording of information means representing the bits of data through ones and zeros. Playing the bits back to again create what was recorded is called digital processing.

DIODE-TRANSISTOR LOGIC (DTL): One of the first bipolar monolithic
IC families of logic gates. A diode in an IC logic gate performs the required logic with a transistor amplifying and inverting the output. The DTL family has been made obsolete by the Transistor-Transistor Logic (TTL) family.

DIRECTORY: A list of files stored in the computer.

DISK: Two distinct types. The names refer to the media inside the container:
A **hard disc** stores vast amounts of data. It is usually inside the computer but can be a separate peripheral on the outside. Hard discs are made up of several rigid coated

metal discs. Currently, hard discs can store 15 to 30 GB (gigabytes)

A **floppy disc**, 3.5" square, usually inserted into the computer and can store about 1.4 megabytes of data. This has become obsolete now.

DIRECT ADDRESS: A memory accessing mode in which the contents of the accessed location is called the OPERAND.

DIRECT MEMORY ACCESS (DMA): A method of transferring blocks of data directly between an external device and the computer system memory without the need for intervention by the CPU. This method significantly speeds up the data transfer rate, improving system efficiency.

DISK DRIVE: The mechanical/electronic section that can accept and operate a compatible floppy or hard disk. It may include several motors (for disk rotation and reading/writing head positioning), position sensors, and control circuits.

DISK MIRRORING: simultaneously storing a copy of information on another disc so that the information can be recovered if the main disc crashes.

DISK STRIPING: storing a bit of information across several discs (instead of storing it all on one disc and hoping that the disc doesn't crash).

DISK OPERATING SYSTEM (DOS): A software program on a disk which coordinates the operation, transfer of data, supervision, and control of a computer. This software program must first be booted into the working memory of the computer from the disk before it can operate.

DISK STORAGE: A method of storing software programs and data on a rotating circular disk (either a floppy or hard disk) coated with magnetic material, such as iron oxide. Data is written (stored) and read (retrieved) by movable read/write heads positioned over data tracks on the surface of the disk. Addressable portions of the disk can be selected for read or write operations.

DISPLAY: A peripheral device serving as a computer readout, such as a cathode-ray tube (CRT), flat-panel (generally for laptop computers), or other readout devices. The screen can be amber, green, or full-color display. Also called a MONITOR.

DNS: This stands for Domain Name System. The Internet runs by assigning different sites "Names." They are actually 4-part strains of numbers associated with names, but names nonetheless. Getting a DNS error means that the address you are attempting to reach is not recognized by the Internet community.

DOCUMENTATION: Information that explains how to use computer hardware or software. It is usually provided as a manual or stored on a disk.

DOMAIN: A domain is a computer, web site or network that is connected to the Internet. A typical domain name looks like this: www.5starsupport.com. The "www" prefix signifies that it is connected to the World Wide Web. The "5starsupport" or body usually indicates the company name and the suffix "com" indicates that it is a commercial site.

DONGLE: A device that attaches to a computer to control access to a particular application. Dongles provide the most effective means of copy protection. The dongle passes through all data coming through the port so it does not prevent the port from being used for other purposes. In fact, it's possible to attach several dongles to the same port.

DOT-MATRIX PRINTER: An impact printer with a computer-driven, multipin print element (print-head). It create images by imprinting a series of tiny dots on a paper to print a wide variety of character styles and/or finely detailed graphics. Generally, these printers are extremely fast and are used for draft-quality documents and precise graphics.

DOTS PER INCH (DPI): The measurement of density on dot-matrix printers or other dot-matrix devices. As the DPI increases, image clarity increases.

DOWNLOAD: The process of transferring information from a web site (or other remote location on a network) to the computer. It is possible to "download a file" or "view a download."

DOWNSTREAM: This refers data that is received from an ISP. Upstream in the data you send back. Some new technology allows for tremendous downstream data transfer rates (100 kilobytes per second or more), but with very slow upstream rates (33.6 kilobits per second or less).

DOWN TIME: A period of time during which a computer is not functioning. It is inoperable because of temporary or permanent failure of hardware or software, or when routine hardware or software maintenance procedures are indicated.

DPI: Stands for Dots Per Inch.

DRIVERS: A driver is a software program that is the driving force behind a device. Each computer device needs a driver. Many drivers are included with a computers operating system when you purchase it.

DROP-DOWN MENU: A menu window that opens vertically on-screen to display context-related options. Also called pop-up menu or pull-down menu.

DSL: Digital Subscriber Line. A method of connecting to the Internet via a phone line. A DSL connection uses copper telephone lines but is able to relay data at much higher speeds than modems and does not interfere with telephone use.

DTP: Desk Top Publisher (ing): A PC Term that describes a program that enables you to design, create and print a variety of projects such as letterheads, birthday cards, calendars, business cards, invitations etc. that would have previously only been possible by using the services of an outside printers business.

DUAL CORE: This refers to a new Central Processing Unit (CPU) structure.
The difference between a single core and dual core is that a dual core system has two CPU's that are electronically wired together. These two CPU's wired together in parallel gives twice the performance than that of its single core counterpart.

DUMB TERMINAL: This a video screen that is seeing manipulation in another computer. Example: If you log in to AOL, your computer is not doing the work — AOL's computer is. You are just being offered a window into that world. That window is your screen. It's a terminal, but it's just watching — thus a dumb terminal.

DVD: Digital Video Disc—Similar to a CD-ROM, it stores and plays both audio and video.

DYNAMIC RANDOM ACCESS MEMORY (DRAM): A type of semiconductor memory in which the presence or absence of a capacitive charge in each element of the memory represents the state of the bit (1 or 0). This charge must be periodically recharged (refreshed) to maintain the desired binary state of the element. See RANDOM ACCESS MEMORY.

E
EBOOK: An electronic (usually hand-held) reading device that allows a person to view digitally stored reading materials.

EBCDIC: Extended Binary Coded Decimal Interchange Code. It is also called the Extended ASCII Code, as it adds an eighth digit to the normal seven digit code.

EDITOR: A program for preparing and/or modifying a SOURCE PROGRAM or other file by addition, deletion, or change.

E-COMMERCE: It means buying or selling any product online using the internet technology. Many companies have set up their web sites which provide the facilities to order and purchase their products and services online.

E-MAIL: (Electronic mail) Messages transmitted over the Internet from user to user. E-mail can contain text, but also can carry with it files of any type as attachments. However, this does NOT guarantee the receiver has the software to open or use the attachment.

E-MAIL SHORTHAND: Over time, Internet e-mailers have come up with their own shorthand to save their time (and energy) and confuse those new to the Internet. Here are some common ones:

BTW: by the way

FWIW: for what it's worth

EMOTICON: A text-based expression of emotion created from ASCII characters that mimics a facial expression when viewed with your head tilted to the left. Here are some examples:

:-) Smiling

:-(Frowning

;-) Winking

:_(Crying

EMITTER-COUPLED LOGIC (ECL): A bipolar monolithic IC logic gate family characterized by very high speed operation and relatively high power dissipation compared with other monolithic IC logic families.

EMULATION: The process of imitation (simulation) of one computer system by another. The imitating program, or device (emulator), accepts the same data, executes the same programs, and achieves the same results.

ENGINE: (as in "Search Engine"): This is the working part of a database or application.

ENCRYPTION: The process of transmitting scrambled data so that only authorized recipients can unscramble it. For instance, encryption is used to scramble credit card information when purchases are made over the Internet.

EPROM (ERASABLE PROGRAMMABLE READ-ONLY MEMORY): A general term for a non-volatile, semiconductor memory that can be programmed, erased, and reprogrammed many times without damage to the device.

ETHERNET: This is a method of file transfer that uses dedicated cables rather than dial up phone lines. Ethernets are usually set up attaching end users to a central system like an Intranet. It was invented by Xerox believe it or not.

ETHERNET CARD: A board inside a computer to which a network cable can be attached.

EVENT: An occurrence during the execution of a task, such as the completion of an input/output operation.

EXECUTE: The command to run a specified instruction or software program.

EXTENDED BINARY CODED DECIMAL INTERCHANGE CODE (EBCDIC): An 8-bit code developed by IBM for their mainframe computers, providing 256 bit-pattern equivalents of standard keyboard symbols.

F

FAQs: (Frequently Asked Questions) Files that are maintained at Internet sites to answer frequently asked questions. INA has a FAQ section for its members.

FAT: Stands for File Allocation Table. Basically this is a table of contents in a directory that tells the computer what al is in there. Look at your Netscape cache, you'll see a FAT. It'll be the first file.

FAN-IN: The maximum number of output terminals from other logic gates that can be connected to an input terminal of a specified logic gate.

FAN-OUT: The maximum number of input terminals that can be connected to the output terminal of a specified logic gate.

FETCH: The command to obtain an instruction from a stored program.

FIBER-OPTIC: This is a new style of cable being used for very high speed data transmission. It works by pushing (modulating) a light wave across cable. The data is carried along with the light.

FILE: A collection of related data treated as a single unit. In a computer, a file can exist on a disk, magnetic tape, or as an accumulation of information in memory.

FILE COMPRESSION: Many computer files can be reduced in size for downloading. Files with .ZIP extension have been "zipped" using PKZip software. Files with .SIT extension have been "stuffed" using Stuffit software. Files with .PDF have also been compressed using Adobe Acrobat. The Acrobat files have the added feature of viewing, printing and placing, using Adobe's Reader program. For example, the Bulletin starts as a 3.5 megabyte file and is compressed to less than 150 kilobytes. That's a compression ratio of almost 24:1

FILE SHARING: This is the most important feature of the Internet. This is a method of allowing one server to give the same file to many different end users.

FIREWALL: A combination of hardware and software that protects a local area network (LAN) from Internet hackers. It separates the network into two or more parts and restricts outsiders to the area "outside" the firewall. Private or sensitive information is kept "inside" the firewall.

FIREWIRE: Apple Computer's high-speed data transfer. Frequently used to import video to a computer.

FIRMWARE: A combination of a software program in hardware, such as a READ-ONLY MEMORY (ROM), or a disk that has files or software programs written on its surface.

FIRST IN, FIRST OUT (FIFO): The term refers to the sequence of entering and then retrieving data from a data storage section of a computer. The first data entered is the first data retrieved.

FLAMES: Insulting, enraged Internet messages.

FLAG: An indicator of a specific condition that informs a section of a program that this condition has already occurred and is identified by the presence or absence of the flag. A flag can be implemented in software and/or hardware.

FLASH MEMORY (FLEXIBLE ARCHITECTURE for SHARED MEMORY): This type of non-volatile memory has the ability to retain its information even when there is no power source. Flash Memory is best known for its use in hand help devices where it is used to store the operating system and core applications. Other devices that use Flash Memory are: Digital Cameras, Audio Players, Cell Phones, Pagers, USB Drives and Printers.

FLIP-FLOP CIRCUIT: A logic circuit having two stable output states. It has the ability to change from one state to the other when an input pulse is applied in a specified manner. It is also called a BISTABLE MULTIVIBRATOR.

FLOATING-POINT ARITHMETIC: A method in which the decimal point location of a number in an arithmetic operation is determined by the number's exponent value in base 10. All exponents are equalized prior to the operation to set a decimal point in its proper location in the final computation. Floating-point arithmetic extends a computer's mathematical capability beyond the limit imposed by a fixed word length and contributes to easier programming.

FLOW CHART: A symbolic representation of the processing steps performed by a software program or a graphic sequence of logic operations implemented in hardware. A flow chart helps to visualize the procedure(s) necessary to design a software program or a final hardware system.

FOLDER: A structure for containing electronic files. In some operating systems, it is called a "directory."

FONTS: Sets of typefaces (or characters) that come in different styles and sizes.

FORMAT: An orderly, structured arrangement of data elements (bits, bytes, and/or fields) that is necessary to produce a larger entity, such as: a list, record, table, file, or dictionary. Also, it is the term that describes the preparation of a magnetic disk to allow it to accept digital data.

FQDN: A **fully qualified domain** name (**FQDN**) is the complete domain name for a specific computer, or host, on the internet. The **FQDN** consists of two parts: the hostname and the domain name. Organizations register names, such as "INAnews.com" or "CNAads.com."

FORTRAN: A science-oriented high-level software language, derived from the contraction of the terms FORmula TRANslator.

FREEWARE Software created by people who are willing to give it away for the satisfaction of sharing or knowing they helped to simplify other people's lives. It may be freestanding software, or it may add functionality to existing software.

FREQUENCY SHIFT KEYING (FSK): A technique of digitally keying (modulating) an audio tone (carrier wave) so that a commercial telephone line can carry digital data. See MODEM.

FTP: (File Transfer Protocol) The basic Internet function that enables files to be transferred between computers. You can use it to download files from a remote, host computer, as well as to upload files from your computer to a remote, host computer. (See Anonymous FTP).

FULL DUPLEX: A data transmission mode that provides simultaneous and independent transmission and reception. A conventional telephone communication is an example of this technique.

G

GATE: See LOGIC GATE.

GATE ARRAY: A group of standard logic gates that can be interconnected into a complete circuit or system. Also called LOGIC ARRAY.

GATEWAY: As in Common Gateway Interface (CGI). It is a piece of software that allows two items to communicate with each other. They are used to make connections between computers and systems inside that computer.

GENERAL PURPOSE INTERFACE BUS (GPIB): A BUS specification standard (IEEE 488) for controlling peripheral devices.

GIF: (Graphics Interchange Format) A graphics file format that is commonly used on the Internet to provide graphics images in Web pages. All graphic files should remain under 5 kilobytes in size to speed page loading. See JPEG and kbps.

GIGABYTE (GB): 1024 megabytes. Also called gig.

GIGO (GARBAGE IN, GARBAGE OUT): The term describing the output of a computer whose operation or accuracy is faulty.

GLITCH: The cause of an unexpected malfunction.

GOPHER: One of the first commonly used interfaces for the Internet with a format structure and resource for providing information. It was created at the University of Minnesota who's mascot is the gopher.

GRAPHICS: Schematic drawings, pictures, line drawings, and/or diagrams generated by data entered into a computer via a keyboard or a data base.

GROUPWARE: Software that allows networked individuals to form groups and collaborate on documents, programs, or databases.

GUI: Graphical User Interface. A system that simplifies selecting computer commands by enabling the user to point to symbols or illustrations (called icons) on the computer screen with a mouse.

H

HACKER: A person with technical expertise who experiments with computer systems to determine how to develop additional features. Hackers are occasionally requested by system administrators to try and "break into" systems via a network to test security. The term hacker is sometimes incorrectly used interchangeably with cracker. A hacker is called a "white hat" and a cracker a "black hat."

HALF-DUPLEX: A communications mode that allows transmission and reception of digital data between computers, but not simultaneously.

HANDSHAKING: The process by which two devices initiate communications.

Handshaking begins when one device sends a message to another device indicating that it wants to establish a communications channel. The two devices then send several messages back and forth that enable them to agree on a communications protocol.

HARD COPY: A paper printout of what you have prepared on the computer.

HARDWARE: The physical and mechanical components of a computer system, such as the electronic circuitry, chips, monitor, disks, disk drives, keyboard, modem, and printer.

HARD-DISK DRIVE: A sealed unit containing high-density, high-speed, rigid metal disks, and recording heads to store digital data. It reads and writes data faster than floppy disks.

HELPER APPLICATION: This is an application your browser uses to manipulate a downloaded program.

HEXADECIMAL: The base 16 number system using 16 symbols (0 to 9 and A to F) to represent 16 decimal numerals (0 to 15).

HIGH-LEVEL LANGUAGE (HLL): A programming language (source code) consisting of a unique group of symbols and command statements representing a series of machine operations. A COMPILER or INTERPRETER translates (converts) a HLL into MACHINE LANGUAGE. BASIC, FORTRAN, PASCAL, ALGOL, and ADA are some examples of high-level languages.

HOME PAGE: The main page of a Web site used to greet visitors, provide information about the site, or to direct the viewer to other pages on the site.

HOST: A computer that "hosts" outside computer users by providing files, services or sharing its resources. INAs Web site is a hosted site. Having a hosted site has the advantage for a company of not having to worry about security, maintenance or upgrading. The disadvantage is a loss of control over these issues, although it is relatively easy to move to a new host.

HOTLIST: List of URLs saved within the Mosaic Web browser. (Bookmark in Netscape.)

HTML (Hypertext Mark-up Language): The basic language that is used to build hypertext documents on the World Wide Web.

HTTP (Hypertext Transfer Protocol): The set of rules (protocol) used by the computers to transfer hypertext documents over the internet.

HYPERTEXT: Text in a document that contains a hidden link to other text. You can click a mouse on a hypertext word and it will take you to the text designated in the link. The wonderful thing about hypertext, however, is its ability to link—using http over the World Wide Web—to any Web document.

HYPERLINK: Text or an image that is connected by hypertext coding to a different location. By selecting the text or image with a mouse, the computer "jumps to" (or displays) the linked text.

HYPERMEDIA: Integrates audio, graphics, and/or video through links embedded in the main program.

I

IBM: Stands for International Business Machines

ICONS: Symbols or illustrations appearing on the computer screen that indicate program files or other computer functions.

IEEE 488: See GENERAL PURPOSE INTERFACE BUS

IMPACT PRINTER: A computer-driven mechanical imprinting device where the characters are formed by the printer-head key striking a ribbon to imprint the character's image onto a paper.

INCREMENT: The increase in the numerical contents of a counter. An increment of one is usually assumed, unless otherwise specified. See
DECREMENT.

INK-JET PRINTER: A printer that forms characters by electrostatically aiming and depositing a tiny patterned drop of ink onto the paper to be printed.

INPUT/OUTPUT (I/O) SECTION: The section that interfaces between the computers' SYSTEM BUS and the peripherals feeding data into and taking data out of the computer. Depending on the number of peripherals in a system, the I/O sections can have a single PORT or multiple ports.

INSTRUCTION: A software statement that specifies a machine operation.
Also called a COMMAND.

INSTRUCTION SET (INSTRUCTION REPERTOIRE): A description of the total operational capabilities of a computer provided by the computer or the CPU (MPU) manufacturer. It consists of a listing of binary words for each executable commands. It is sometimes called the computer's MICROCODE.

INTERPRETER: A high-level language translator that converts individual High level computer language program instructions (source code) into machine instructions. It translates and executes each statement line-byline during the running of the program.

INTERRUPT: The suspension of normal program execution to perform a higher priority service routine as requested by a peripheral device. After completion of the service routine operation, the interrupted program routine is resumed at the point where it was interrupted.

INTERNET: Established in the 1960s by the US government, the Internet was developed so that government agencies and universities could link research centres in response the perceived notion that the Soviet Union was becoming more advanced in the space race. The Internet was created as a "decentralized" network, meaning that there is no one place that makes up the

Internet. This was done to make sure the Internet survived a nuclear war. Today, the Internet is a vast collection of e-mail, Usenet groups, FTP sites, and Web sites, with millions upon millions of users from around the world.

INTERNET PIRACY: Unauthorized copies downloaded over the internet falls under internet piracy.

INTERNET SERVICE PROVIDER (ISP): It is a company which provides Internet access to its customers.

INTERFACE: This is any type of point where two different things come together. Most often, the term is used to describe the programs between you and your computer like Windows, OS/2 and others. What you see on the screen is the interface between you and what your computer is doing.

INPUT: Data that goes into a computer device.

INPUT DEVICE: A device, such as a keyboard, stylus and tablet, mouse, puck, or microphone, which allows input of information (letters, numbers, sound, video) to a computer.

INSTANT MESSENGING (IM): A chat application that allows two or more people to communicate over the Internet via real-time keyed-in messages.

IP: (Internet Protocol) The rules that provide basic Internet functions. (See
TCP/IP).

IP (INTERNET PROTOCOL) ADDRESS: An Internet Protocol address is a unique set of numbers used to locate another computer on a network. The format of an IP address is a 32-bit string of four numbers separated by periods. Each number can be from 0 to 255 (i.e., 1.154.10.266). Within a closed network IP addresses may be assigned at random, however, IP addresses of web servers must be registered to avoid duplicates.

IRC: (Internet Relay Chat) Currently an Internet tool with a limited use that lets users join a "chat" channel and exchange typed, text messages. Few people have used IRC, but it is going to create a revolution in communication when the Internet can provide the bandwidth to carry full-color, live action video and audio. IRC came into its own during the Gulf War where unbiased reports of the war were sent back to the United States using Internet Relay Chat to get around US military censors.

ISDN: (Integrated Services Digital Network) A set of communications standards that enable a single phone line or optical cable to carry voice, digital network services and video.

ISO: Stands for the International Standards Organization or International Organization for Standardization. They assign standards to various companies and organisations.

J
JAVA: Java is a programming language, which allows a programmer to write the code once on their computer

platform and is then usable on any Javaware computer platform.

JAVA SCRIPT: This is a language very close to Java that allows for more interaction with the viewer.

JPEG: (Joint Photographic Experts Group) The name of the committee that designed the photographic image-compression standard. JPEG is optimized for compressing full-color or gray-scale photographic-type, digital images. Photos are generally stored in JPEG format on the Internet. All graphics files should remain very small with an option for the user to view a larger photo. Graphics are stored in GIF format.

JUGHEAD: Search browser like "Archie".

JUMP: An instruction that causes the computer to fetch the next instruction to be executed from a location other than the next sequential location in memory.

K

KEYBOARD: A peripheral device consisting of alphanumerics, punctuation marks, and other special function keys that are mechanically arranged to allow the entry of data, commands, and other information into the system.

K OR KBPS: (kilobits per second). A speed rating for computer modems that measures (in units of 1,024 bits) the maximum number of bits the device can transfer in one second under ideal conditions.

KILOBYTE (KB) This is about a thousand bytes of space. In reality, it's two to the 10th power or 1,024 bytes.

L

LANDSCAPE: A printer feature, generally controlled by software, which rotates the output image by 90° to print across the length rather than the width of the paper.

LAPTOP AND NOTEBOOK: Small, lightweight, portable battery-powered\ computers that can fit onto your lap. They each have a thin, flat, liquid crystal display screen.

LASER (LIGHT AMPLIFICATION by STIMULATED EMISSION of RADIATION): A system that generates high-intensity, highly-focused light for many purposes, including printers, high-density memory media, and a light generator for fiber optic transmission systems.

LASER DISK: See CD-ROM

LASER PRINTER: A computer-driven photocopier that creates an original image of the text or graphics from the output of the computer. A computer controlled laser beam "paints" the desired image inside the photocopier and then prints the image on a sheet of paper.

LAST-IN, FIRST-OUT (LIFO): A method of storing and retrieving data in a stack, table, or list.

LEASED LINE: A leased phone line that provides a full-time, dedicated, direct connection to the Internet.

LIBRARY: A collection of standard software instructions, programs, routines, and subroutines in a computer's memory.

LIGHT PEN: A light-sensitive stylus for forming graphics by touching coordinates on a display screen, thereby seeming to draw directly on the screen.

LINK: See hyperlink.

LINKAGE: Instructions that connect one program to another, providing continuity of executions between the programs.

LINUX: A UNIX like, open-source operating system developed primarily by
Linus Torvalds. Linux is free and runs on many platforms, including both
PCs and Macintoshes.

LIST SERVE: An Internet application that automatically "serves" mailing lists by sending electronic newsletters to a stored database of Internet user addresses. Users can handle their own subscribe/unsubscribe actions without requiring anyone at the server location to personally handle the transaction.

LIVE SCRIPT: This is the former name of Java Script. There are few updates between the two.

LOCAL AREA NETWORK (LAN): A combined hardware/software technique for interconnecting company related multiple computers or computer terminals through a high-speed networking system.

LOGIC GATE: A digital circuit resulting in an output whose state (0 or 1) depends on the specific combination of the states of input signals.

Definitions of the more commonly used logic gates are listed below:

- **AND:** All inputs must be in a "1" state to produce a "1" state output.
- **NAND (NOT AND):** All inputs must be in a "1" state to produce a "0" state output.
- **NOR (NOT OR):** Any one input, or more, in a "1" state will produce a "0" state output.
- **NOT (INVERTER):** A logic gate having only one input and one output. If the input is in a "1" state, the output is in a "0" state and vice versa.
- **OR:** Any one input, or more, in a "1" state will produce a "1" state at the output.
- **XOR (EXCLUSIVE OR):** If any of the inputs are in a "1" state, but not if two or more inputs are "1", the output is in a "1" state.
- **LOOK AHEAD:** 1. A feature of a CPU which allows the masking of an interrupt request until the current sequential instruction has been completed.

- A feature of an adder circuit in the ALU section which allows the
  circuit to look ahead to see that all the generated arithmetic carries are
  available for addition.
- **LOOPING:** The repetition of program instructions until a conditional exit situation is encountered.
- **LOGIN:** To attach to a computer. It has also come to represent your User ID command.
- **LOGIN SCRIPT:** This is the small text file that is run by the server gateway to make the attachment between it and your computer.

M

MACHINE LANGUAGE: Sets of numeric binary code instructions in a computer which execute its operations. All other programming languages (SOURCE PROGRAMS) must be translated into machine language (OBJECT PROGRAM) before entering the CPU.

MACRO: A combination of commands, instructions, or keystrokes which may be stored in a computer's memory to be executed as a single command by a single keystroke or a simultaneous combination of keystrokes.

MACROASSEMBLER: An assembly language translator that converts macro expressions into several machine language instructions. Although macros simplify program coding and speed up execution of a program, a code for each macro must also be generated.

MAC OS: An operating system with a graphical user interface, developed by

Apple for Macintosh computers. Current System "X.1" (10) combines the traditional Mac interface with a strong underlying UNIX? Operating system for increased performance and stability.

MAILING LIST: An e-mail based discussion group. Sending one e-mail message to the mailing list's list server sends mail to all other members of the group. Users join a mailing list by subscribing. Subscribers to a mailing list receive messages from all other members. Users have to unsubscribe from a mailing list to stop receiving messages forwarded from the group's members.

MALWARE: The adware designed to monitor your keyboard keystrokes so that the author of the software can gain access to your password protected accounts are referred to as "malware" due to its malicious intent.

MEGABYTE (MB): About a million bytes of space. Actually it's 2 raised to the 20th power or 1,048,576 bytes of space.

MEMORY: Temporary storage for information, including applications and documents. The information must be stored to a permanent device, such as a hard disc or CD-ROM before the power is turned off, or the information will be lost. Computer memory is measured in terms of the amount of information it can store, commonly in megabytes or gigabytes.

MENU: A context-related list of options that users can choose from.

MENU BAR: The horizontal strip across the top of an application's window. Each word on the strip has a context sensitive drop-down menu containing features and actions that are available for the application in use.

MERGE: To combine two or more files into a single file.

MHz: An abbreviation for Megahertz, or one million hertz. One MHz represents one million clock cycles per second and is the measure of a computer microprocessor's speed. For example, a microprocessor that runs at 300 MHz executes 300 million cycles per second. Each instruction a computer receives takes a fixed number of clock cycles to carry out, therefore the more cycles a computer can execute per second, the faster its programs run. Megahertz is also a unit of measure for bandwidth.

MICROPROCESSOR: A complete central processing unit (CPU) contained on a single silicon chip.

MINIMIZE: A term used in a GUI operating system that uses windows. It refers to reducing a window to an icon, or a label at the bottom of the screen, allowing another window to be viewed.

MICROCOMPUTER: A microprocessor-based computer, consisting of an
MPU, internal semiconductor memory, input and output sections, and a system bus, all on one, or several monolithic IC chips inserted into one or several PC boards. The addition of a power supply and connecting cables, appropriate peripherals (keyboard, monitor, printer, disk drives, etc.), an operating system and other software

programs can provide a complete microcomputer system. The microcomputer is generally the smallest of the computer family, however, the improvement in performance capability of newer microcomputer systems can make the microcomputer as powerful as larger systems.

MICROPROCESSOR UNIT (MPU): The Central Processor Unit (CPU) implemented in monolithic IC technology, usually, but not necessarily, on one VLSI chip. In many cases, the SYSTEM BUS is also included on the MPU chip.

MIDI: Stands for Music Instrument Digital Interface. It allows a computer to store and replay a musical instrument's output.

MINICOMPUTER: Considered to be more capable than a microcomputer but less powerful than a mainframe. Generally, the WORD-WIDTH of the minicomputer is between 12 to 32 bits.

MIME (Multipurpose Internet Mail Extensions): A set of Internet functions that extends normal e-mail capabilities and enables computer files to be attached to e-mail. Files sent by MIME arrive at their destination as exact copies of the original so that you can send fully-formatted word processing files, spread sheets, graphics images and software applications to other users via simple e-mail. Aladdin's Stuffit Expander will automatically convert MIME files.

MNEMONIC: A symbolic label or code reminder that assists the user in remembering a specific operation or command.
See ASSEMBLY LANGUAGE.

MODEL: A representation of a process or system that can be controlled to demonstrate the effects that various actions will have on the process or system.

MONITOR: The visual readout device of a computer system. A monitor can be in several forms: a cathode ray tube (CRT), a liquid crystal display (LCD), or a flat-panel, full-color display. See DISPLAY.

MODEM: A device that connects two computers together over a telephone or cable line by converting the computer's data into an audio signal. Modem is a contraction for the process it performs: modulate-demodulate.

MOSAIC: The first Web browser to have a consistent interface for the Macintosh, Windows, and UNIX environments. It was created at the National Center for Supercomputing Applications (NCSA). The success of this browser is really responsible for the expansion of the Web.

MOUSE: A small hand-held device, similar to a trackball, used to control the position of the cursor on the video display; movements of the mouse on a desktop correspond to movements of the cursor on the screen.

MP3: Stands for MPEG (Moving Picture Expert Group) Audio Layer 3. This is a compression standard that was developed to create a small audio file size while keeping a high quality sound. The small file size allows the sound to be streamed or downloaded over the Internet with ease.

MP4: Stands for MPEG (Moving Picture Expert Group): 4. Finalized toward the end of 1998, this became an International Standard in the beginning of 1999. This was developed to provide low bandwidth multimedia applications.

MPEG: Stands for Motion Picture Experts Group. A format to make, view, and transfer both digital audio and digital video files.

MULTITASKING: The technique of using several applications programs (tasks) in a computer system or on several terminals in a network at the same time. Multitasking can simultaneously work with several programs or interrelated tasks that share memories, codes, buffers, and files.

MULTIUSER: The term describing the capability of a computer system to be operated at more than one terminal at the same time.

MULTIPLEXER This is a piece of hardware that allows one item to take the place of several. An example would be using a multiplexer to allow 10 computers to attach where only one could before.

MULTIMEDIA: Software programs that combine text and graphics with sound, video, and animation. A **multimedia PC** contains the hardware to support these capabilities.

N

NACS: Stands for Netware Asynchronous Communication Services.

NEGATIVE LOGIC: This term refers to logic in which the negative voltage represents the "1" state and the zero voltage represents the "0" state.
See POSITIVE LOGIC.

NESTING: Embedding commands or data in levels of other data so that specific routines or instructions can be executed or accessed continuously in loops, without returning to the main program.

NETSCAPE NAVIGATOR: Currently the dominant World Wide Web browser. Information on the latest version of the browser can be found at www.netscape.com.

NETWORK ADAPTER: This is the hardware that allows the computers that are part of a network to communicate with each other.

NETWORK: A system of interconnected computers.

NEWBIE: An inexperienced newcomer to the Internet.

NIBBLE: A sequence of four adjacent bits, or a half-byte.
A hexadecimal or
BCD coded digit can be represented by a nibble.

NODE: The endpoint of a network branch or the junction of two or more branches.

NON-VOLATILE MEMORY: A memory where stored data remains undisturbed by the removal of electrical power.

O

OBJECT: Something that contains both the data and the application that operates on that data.

OBJECT CODE: Machine language code produced by a translator program, such as an assembler, interpreter, or compiler. Instructions in object code can be executed by a Central Processing Unit (CPU). See SOURCE CODE.

OOP: Stands for Object Oriented Program. A larger program made up of smaller objects.

OPEN SOURCE: Computer programs whose original source code was revealed to the general public so that it could be developed openly. Software licensed as open source can be freely changed or adapted to new uses, meaning that the source code of the operating system is freely available to the public. Programmers may redistribute and modify the code, as long as they don't collect royalties on their work or deny access to their code. Since development is not restricted to a single corporation more programmers can debug and improve the source code faster.

OPERATING SYSTEM: A set of instructions that tell a computer on how to operate when it is turned on. It sets up a filing system to store files and tells the computer how to display information on a video display. Most PC operating systems are DOS (disc operated system) systems, meaning the instructions are stored on a disc (as opposed to being originally stored in the microprocessors of the computer). Other well-known operating systems include UNIX, Linux, Macintosh, and Windows.

OPERATION CODE (OP-CODE): Part of a computer instruction word that designates the function performed by a specific instruction. For example, op-codes for arithmetic instructions include: "ADD", "SUB", "MUL" and "DIV".

OUTPUT: Data that come out of a computer device. For example, information displayed on the monitor, sound from the speakers, and information printed to paper.

OVERFLOW: An error condition occurring in a computer when a mathematical operation produces a result having a magnitude that exceeds the capacity of the computer's arithmetic register.

P
PALMTOP: A hand-held computer.

PASCAL: A high-level programming language that is structured to encourage efficient programming habits (documentation) and is used extensively in educational institutions and engineering environments.

PARALLEL OPERATION: A method of data transmission in which all bits\ of a digital word are handled simultaneously with each bit on a separate line. Although faster and simpler to install and operate than SERIAL OPERATION, this method requires more transmission lines (real estate).

PARITY: A method of verifying the accuracy of binary data after it has been transferred to or from a storage area.

PARTITION: A portion of a hard disk that functions as a separate unit. A single hard disk can be divided into several partitions, each of which functions as a separate drive and has its own volume name (such as D:, E:, F:, and so on). The purpose is to make the drive more efficient, as the computer can search smaller sections for a specific file rather than the entire drive. The verb to partition refers to the process of dividing the hard drive into partitions.

PC BOARD: Printed Circuit board. A board printed or etched with a circuit and processors. Power supplies, information storage devices, or changers are attached.

PCMCIA (PERSONAL COMPUTER MEMORY CARD INTERNATIONAL ASSOCIATION): A package in a plastic card form containing semiconductor memory, particularly FLASH. These cards are plugged into the card slot in laptop computers.

PDA: Personal Digital Assistant. A hand-held computer that can store daily appointments, phone numbers, addresses, and other important information. Most PDAs link to a desktop or laptop computer to download or upload information.

PDF: Stands for Portable Document Format. A technology developed by Adobe and was designed to capture all of the elements of a printed document and place it in a single image file. This PDF file can be navigated, printed or attached to an email for sharing. In order to be able to view a PDF file on your computer, you will need to download and install the free Acrobat Reader. Once installed, anytime a PDF file is clicked, the image file will automatically be viewed.

PEER TO PEER: A type of network in which each workstation has equivalent capabilities and responsibilities. This differs from client/server architectures, in which some computers are dedicated to serving the others. Peer-to-peer networks are generally simpler and less expensive, but they usually do not offer the same performance under heavy loads.

PEN DRIVE: A small key ring-sized device that can be used to easily transfer files between USB-compatible systems. Available in a range of capacities (and in some cases, with an MP3 player built-in). Plug it in to any USB port and it will be automatically detected by the Operating System.

PENTIUM CHIP: Intel's fifth generation of sophisticated high-speed microprocessors. Pentium means "the fifth element."

PERIPHERAL: A term designating the various kinds of machines and devices that work in conjunction with a computer but are not necessarily part of the computer structure. Typically, peripherals refer to: printers, keyboards, monitors, scanners, CD ROM drives, and plotters. A hard drive, floppy disk drive, and a MODEM are considered to be peripheral devices even though they may be physically located inside a computer.

PERSONAL COMPUTER (PC): A single-user computer containing a central processing unit (CPU) and one or more memory circuits.

PETABYTE: A measure of memory or storage capacity and is approximately a thousand terabytes.

PETAFLOP: A theoretical measure of a computer's speed and can be expressed as a thousand-trillion floating-point operations per second.

PICT: It is another image format.

PLATFORM: The operating system, such as UNIX□, Macintosh□, Windows, on which a computer is based.

PLUG-IN: This is a program that your browser uses to manipulate a downloaded file. It differs from a Helper Application in that the plug-in works inside the browser window.

PLUG AND PLAY: Computer hardware or peripherals that come set up with necessary software so that when attached to a computer, they are "recognized" by the computer and are ready to use.

PLUG-COMPATIBLE: A term that describes the ability of peripherals to be interchanged without modification.

POLLING: A process in which a number of peripheral devices, remote stations, or nodes in a computer network are interrogated, one at a time, to determine if service is required.

POP (Post Office Protocol): An Internet protocol that enables a single user to read e-mail from a mail server.

POP (Point of Presence): A site that has an array of telecommunications equipment: modems, digital, leased lines and Internet routers. An Internet access provider may operate several regional PoPs to provide Internet connections within local phone service areas. An alternative is for access providers to employ virtual PoPs (virtual Points of Presence) in conjunction with third party provider.

POP-UP MENU: A menu window that opens vertically or horizontally onscreen to display context-related options. Also called drop-down menu or pull-down menu.

PORT: An input/output channel (either parallel or serial), terminated at a connector on the computer. It interconnects the computer's input and/or output terminals to an appropriate source and/or destination.

PORTRAIT: A term that designates the position of conventional printing across the width of a page.

POSITIVE LOGIC: This logic represents the reverse of NEGATIVE LOGIC.
It is the more commonly used form of logic. A positive voltage represents a "1" state and a negative (or zero) voltage represents a "0" state.

POWER PC: A competitor of the Pentium chip. It is a new generation of powerful sophisticated microprocessors produced from an Apple- IBM Motorola alliance.

PPP: Stands for Point To Point Protocol. It's a software application that allows an attachment to a server.

PRINT SPOOLER: A device for temporarily storing data to be printed when the printer is functioning. It provides uninterrupted data entry and editing while\ the printer is active and while other data awaits transmission to the printer.

PRINTER: A mechanical device for printing a computer's output on paper.

PROGRAM: A complete sequence of computer software instructions necessary to provide an application, solve a specific problem, perform an action, or respond to external stimuli in a prescribed manner. As a verb, it means to develop a program.

PROGRAM COUNTER (PC): A special-purpose register in the CPU which contains the address of the next instruction to be fetched and executed.

PROGRAMMABLE LOGIC ARRAY (PLA): An unprogrammed, general purpose logic structure in monolithic IC form consisting of an array of similar, and/or compatible logic gates. Also called PROGRAMMABLE ARRAY LOGIC (PAL).

PROGRAMMABLE READ-ONLY MEMORY (PROM): A blank read-only memory (ROM) that is programmed with external programming equipment after manufacture. Once programmed, it is not re-programmable and is considered to be a ROM.

PROGRAMMING LANGUAGE: A series of instructions written by a programmer according to a given set of rules or conventions ("syntax"). High-level programming languages are independent of the device on which the application (or program) will eventually run; low-level languages are specific to each program or platform. Programming language instructions are converted into programs in language specific to a particular machine or operating system ("machine language") so that the computer can interpret and carry out the instructions. Some common programming languages are BASIC, C, C++, dBASE, FORTRAN, and Perl.

PROPAGATION DELAY: The time required for the output of a logic gate to respond to a combination of input pulses.

PROTOCOLS: Computer rules that provide uniform specifications so that computer hardware and operating systems can communicate. It's similar to the way that mail, in countries around the world, is addressed in the same basic format so that postal workers know where to find the recipient's address, the sender's return address and the postage stamp. Regardless of the underlying language, the basic "protocols" remain the same.

PROXY-SERVER: A server that acts as an intermediary between a workstation user and the internet so that the enterprise can ensure security, administrative control, and caching service. A proxy server is associated with, or part of, a gateway server that separates the enterprise network from the outside network and a firewall server that protects the enterprise network from the outside intrusion.

PUCK: An input device, like a mouse. It has a magnifying glass with crosshairs on the front of it that allows the operator to position it precisely when tracing a drawing for use with CAD-CAM software.

PULL-DOWN MENU: A menu window that opens vertically on-screen to display context-related options. Also called drop-down menu or pop-up menu.

PUSH: The instruction used to deposit a word on top of a stack.

PUSH-DOWN STACK: A dedicated temporary storage register in a computer, sometimes part of a system memory, structured so that data (words) in the stack are retrieved in reverse order of entry. See LIFO.

PUSH TECHNOLOGY: Internet tool that delivers specific information directly to a user's desktop, eliminating the need to surf for it. PointCast, which delivers news in user-defined categories, is a popular example of this technology.

Q

QUERY: This is to make a computer request of a database.

QUICK-TIME PLAYER: A multimedia technology developed by Apple
Computer. Developed to display video, sound, animation, graphics, text, music and 360 degree virtual reality (VR) scenes. Apple makes its QuickTime plug-in available for free and once installed on your computer system, you can watch streaming media within a web page.

R

RAID: Redundant Array of Inexpensive Disks. A method of spreading information across several disks set up to act as a unit, using two different techniques.

RAM: Random Access Memory. One of two basic types of memory. Portions of programs are stored in RAM when the program is launched so that the program will run faster. Though a PC has a fixed amount of RAM, only portions of it will be accessed by the computer at any given time. Also called memory.

RAM DISK (DISK EMULATOR): A portion of a hard drive configured to emulate a RAM. It accesses information quickly, but its data must be saved in a non-volatile memory for future use. Otherwise, the information is lost when power is removed.

RANDOM ACCESS: A technique of accessing (reading) a word of data from a memory structure by the CPU. Since a word in the memory can be accessed directly, the time required is independent of its location (address) in the memory structure. It is sometimes called a "direct access" method.

RANDOM ACCESS MEMORY (RAM): A volatile, semiconductor storage structure that accesses temporary data with a random or direct accessing method. It is more accurately referred to as "erasable read/write" memory. Data in this memory can be read by the CPU, edited, altered, erased, or new information written over existing data by computer commands. Its data must be saved for future access by writing it into a non-volatile memory. See NON-VOLATILE MEMORY and VOLATILE MEMORY.

READ-ONLY MEMORY (ROM): A semiconductor memory whose data cannot be erased, or overwritten; it can only be accessed (read) for use by the CPU. The data in a ROM is of a permanent nature and is programmed by the ROM manufacturer. In many cases, its programmed information identifies the dedicated function of a computer. A ROM can also be in the physical form of a module (tape or disk) that is plugged into a computer to change its operation from one program to another.

REALAUDIO: This is a method of playing sounds invented by Rob Glasser that creates a buffer between the supplying server and your computer. The file is played without downloading it completely.

REAL TIME: This is method of processing data the moment it is received. Batch mode is a term used for a mainframe computer dealing with data when it has the time.

REAL-TIME DATA: Time-dependent data processed by a computer whose output data is capable of controlling other time-related events, such as traffic control. Real time is the actual time it takes for an event to occur.

REBOOT: To restart a computer. In DOS, you can reboot by pressing the Alt,
Control and Delete keys simultaneously. This is called a warm boot. You can also perform a cold boot by turning the computer off and then on again. On Macs, you reboot by selecting the "Restart" option from the Special menu.

REFRESH: Generally, to update something with new data. For example, some
Web browsers include a refresh button that updates the currently display Web pages. This feature is also called reload. To recharge a device with power or information. For example, dynamic RAM needs to be refreshed thousands of times per second or it will lose the data stored in it. Similarly, display monitors must be refreshed many times per second. The refresh rate for a monitor is measured in hertz (Hz) and is also called the vertical frequency, vertical scan rate, frame rate or vertical refresh rate. The old standard for monitor refresh rates was 60Hz, but a new standard developed by VESA sets the refresh rate at 75Hz for monitors displaying resolutions of 640x480 or greater. This means that the monitor redraws the display 75 times per second. The faster the refresh rate, the less the monitor flickers.

REGISTER: A temporary storage unit for quick, direct accessibility of a small amount of data for processing. Most computers include a set of internal registers that can be accessed more quickly than the system's main memory.

RESIDENT SOFTWARE: The program(s) residing in the main memory of a computer system. For convenience of operation, several software programs can reside in RAM after the computer is turned on and booted, and they can be accessed quickly from within another program.

RESOLUTION: Refers to the sharpness and clarity of an image. The term is most often used to describe monitors, printers, and bit-mapped graphic images. In the case of dot-matrix and laser printers, the resolution indicates the number of dots per inch. For example, a 300-dpi (dots per inch) printer is one that is capable of printing 300 distinct dots in a line 1 inch long. This means it can print 90,000 dots per square inch.

RS-232-C: Identifies an interconnection standard for serial operation. It specifies the configuration and type of connectors in the computer's serial I/O port(s) and peripheral serial port(s).

ROUTER: A network device that enables the network to reroute messages it receives that are intended for other networks. The network with the router receives the message and sends it on its way exactly as received. In normal operations, they do not store any of the messages that they pass through.

RIGHT-CLICK: Using the right mouse button to open context-sensitive dropdown menus.

S

SATA: Serial Advanced Technology Attachment. A computer bus designed to transfer data to and from a hard drive using serial signalling technology. Because SATA cables are thinner than its ribbon type counterpart, they can be connected to more devices while maintaining its signal integrity.

SCANNER: An electronic device that uses light-sensing equipment to scan paper images such as text, photos, and illustrations and translate the images into signals that the computer can then store, modify, or distribute.

SCRATCH PAD MEMORY: A group of internal registers used for the temporary storage of data being collected and sorted for immediate processing. It is analogous to a pad of paper for quickly jotting down notes.

SDRAM: Short for "Synchronous Dynamic Random Access Memory". This is a newer type of DRAM that has the ability to run at much higher clock speeds than conventional memory.

SEARCH ENGINE: It is a programme that makes it possible to look for and retrieve material on the Internet, particularly the Web. The most popular search engine is Google.

SERVER: A computer that shares its resources and information with other computers, called clients, on a network.

SERIAL: This is a consecutive occurrence of two items in the same channel.

SECTOR: A section of a recording track on a magnetic disk.

SEMICONDUCTOR MEMORY: Data storage devices formed with semiconductor components (generally monolithic ICs). See RAM, ROM, PROM, EPROM, EAPROM, EEPROM, and FLASH.

SERIAL OPERATION: A method of data transmission where the data is handled in sequence, one bit at a time. See PARALLEL OPERATION.

SERVICE ROUTINE: A set of instructions for performing a programmed operation, typically, in response to an interrupt command.

SERVER: This is a mainframe computer that serves the other computers attached to it.

SHAREWARE: Software created by people who are willing to sell it at low\ cost or no cost for the gratification of sharing. It may be freestanding software, or it may add functionality to existing software.

SHAREWARE: This is an application that a programmer makes available to users for a set amount of time and then asks for a donation. In return for the donation, a registration number is often returned that can be used to "turn on" the features of the program.

SHELL ACCOUNT: A software application that lets you use someone else's Internet connection. It's not the same as having your own, direct Internet connection, but pretty close. Instead, you connect to a host computer and use the Internet through the host computer's connection. Most users connect via shell accounts because of the current high cost to have direct Internet access.

SHELL: This is a program that sets parameters and acts as a series of boundaries in which an application can run.

SHIFT: A computer operation consisting of moving a group of adjacent data bits either to the left or to the right by a prescribed number of positions. The move is done in a SHIFT REGISTER for a carry-over operation.

SIGNATURE FILE: An ASCII text file, maintained within e-mail programs, that contains a few lines of text for your signature. The programs automatically attach the file to your messages so you don't have to repeatedly type a closing.

SIMPLEX: A data transmission mode that provides transmission in one direction only.
See FULL DUPLEX and HALF DUPLEX.

SIMULATION: The imitation of a logical operation of one computer by another to measure and evaluate the operation of the computer being designed. Simulation is primarily intended to provide an analysis of program logic, independent of hardware environment, and is extremely useful for debugging a new software program prior to committing it to ROM.

SKYPE: This is a peer-to-peer voice over Internet protocol (VoIP). This Internet telephony network was created by the same people that created Kazaa (Niklas Zennström and Janus Friis). It was developed as a free desktop software application that gives users the ability to make free Internet phone calls to other Skype users or you can use the application to place and receive phone calls to and from traditional phone lines for a reduced fee.

SLIP/PPP: (Serial Line Internet Protocol/Point-to-Point Protocol) The basic rules that enable computers to connect, usually by dial-up modem, directly to other computers that provide Internet services.

SMTP: (Simple Mail Transfer Protocol) The basic programming language behind the Internet's e-mail functions. SMTP is poised for a major upgrade, because it doesn't provide such simple information as unsend or e-mail status.

SOCIAL NETWORKING: Social Networking is an online community of internet users. It provides a virtual community in which the members with common interests may communicate with each other. Facebook, Orkut are two most popular Social Networking Sites.

SOFTWARE: This is a program, the actual code the computer reads. All other stuff is hardware.

SOURCE CODE (SOURCE PROGRAM): A set of computer instructions in hard-copy or stored form. When written in a language other than machine language, the source code requires translation by an assembler (or macro assembler), interpreter, or compiler into object code.

SPIDER: A process search engines use to investigate new pages on a web site and collect the information that needs to be put in their indices.

SPREADSHEET: Software that allows one to calculate numbers in a format that is similar to pages in a conventional ledger.

SPAM: This is to transmit unwanted messages, usually over email, to a great many people.

SPOOFING: To fool. In networking, the term is used to describe a variety of ways in which hardware and software can be fooled. Email spoofing, for example, involves trickery that makes a message appear as if it came from a legitimate business email address.

SPOOLING: The process of storing a device (eg: printer) output signal in a queue, while the device can take on other actions. When the device is ready to take on other actions, it will draw from the queue. The term spooling is derived from the acronym "Spool": Simultaneous Peripheral Operations On-Line.

STATE: The logic input or output condition of a binary digital circuit: the state is either a "0" or "1".

STACK: A dynamic, sequential data list usually contained in the computer system's main memory. It has special provisions to access data from either end. Storage and retrieval of data from the stack is performed automatically by the CPU.

STATIC MEMORY: A type of semiconductor read/write memory (RAM) that does not require periodic refresh cycles. As long as electrical power is ON, the data in a static memory is maintained.

STORAGE: Devices used to store massive amounts of information so that it can be readily retrieved. Devices include RAIDs, CD-ROMs, DVDs.

STREAMING: Taking packets of information (sound or visual) from the Internet and storing it in temporary files to allow it to play in continuous flow.

STYLUS AND TABLET: A input device similar to a mouse. The stylus is pen shaped. It is used to "draw" on a tablet (like drawing on paper) and the tablet transfers the information to the computer. The tablet responds to pressure—the firmer the pressure used to draw, the thicker the line appears.

STORAGE CAPACITY: The amount of data that can be retained in a memory unit. It is expressed either by a number of bits or bytes (8-bit words).

STREAMER/STREAMING TAPES: A small tape recorder, usually in cassette form, is used to store data from a hard disk for the purpose of backing up this data.

SUBROUTINE: A short program segment that performs a specific function and is available for general use by other programs and routines.

SUPERCOMPUTER: The largest mainframe computer featuring exceptionally high speed operation while manipulating huge amounts of information.

SUPPORT CHIPS: Computer-related circuits other than the CPU. Examples are: main memory (RAM and ROM), I/O ports, and system bus.

SURFING: Exploring the Internet.

SURGE PROTECTOR: A controller to protect the computer and make up for variances in voltage.

SVGA: Stands for Super Video Graphics Adapter. It's a high level monitor.

SYNCHRONOUS COMMUNICATION: A method of transferring binary data, in serial form, between computers or between a computer and its peripherals. Transmission of data is at a rate set by the computer's clock with synchronization bits located at the beginning of each message or block of data.

SYNTAX: A set of grammatical rules defining valid use of specific commands or instructions in a computer language.

SYSTEMS SOFTWARE: A general term for software that supervises, sequences, and coordinates programs. Systems software may include programs, such as: operating systems, assemblers, interpreters, compilers, software debugging programs, text editors, utilities and peripheral drivers.

T

T1: An Internet backbone line that carries up to 1.536 million bits per second (1.536Mbps).

T3: An Internet line that carries up to 45 million bits per second (45Mbps).
That's 160 times as fast as a 28.8k modem!

TCP/IP: Stands for Transmission Control Protocol/Internet Protocol. This is a large grouping of programs and standards that govern how information moves round the Internet. The protocols were established around 1970- 1980 to allow computers to attach to one another.

TERABYTE (TB): It's about a trillion bytes. Actually it's 2 to the 40th power or 1,009,511,627,776 bytes.

TERAFLOP: A measure of a computer's speed. It can be expressed as a trillion floating-point operations per second.

TERMINAL: This is what you look at when you're on the Internet. It's your computer screen.

TERMINAL EMULATION: This is an application that allows your terminal to act as a dumb terminal.

TEXT EDITOR: See EDITOR.

TELNET: An Internet protocol that let you connect your computer as a remote workstation to a host computer anywhere in the world and to use that computer as if you were logged on locally.

THIRD-PARTY SOFTWARE: Software developed by a software company rather than by a computer manufacturer or user.

THREAD: In online discussions, a series of messages that have been posted as replies to each other. A single forum or conference typically contains many threads covering different subjects. By reading each message in a thread, one after the other, you can see how the discussion has evolved. You can start a new thread by posting a message that is not a reply to an earlier message.

THROUGHPUT: The number of instructions executed per second, measured in millions of instructions per second (MIPS) or billions of instructions per second (BIPS).

TOGGLE: To switch back and forth between two states or conditions of operation, as in a toggle switch.

TOP-DOWN HIERARCHICAL DESIGN: A hardware and/or software design approach that starts at the most general level of a machine or software program. It proceeds, step-by-step, to lower levels, adding detail as the design progresses.

TRACK: A ring on the surface of a magnetic disk.

TRACKBALL: Input device that controls the position of the cursor on the screen; the unit is mounted near the keyboard, and movement is controlled by moving a ball.

TRACTOR-FEED: A pin-fed device for advancing continuous form paper through a computer printer.

TRANSISTOR-TRANSISTOR LOGIC (T2L): A logic gate family that provides higher-speed and higher-power than the obsolete DTL logic family.
The first transistor in the circuit performs the required logic. Another transistor amplifies and inverts the output. Improved pin-compatible versions of this logic family are called TTL-Schottky (T2L-S) and Low Power TTLS (LPT2L-S).

TRANSLATOR: See ASSEMBLER, MACROASSEMBLER, INTERPRETER, and COMPILER.

TRANSPARENT: Something that occurs without being known to the user.

TRI-STATE LOGIC: The term that designates the possible conditions of a specific logic gate output: "0", "1" or "undefined".

TROJAN: A type of computer virus that is loaded into an unsuspecting users system via a host program such as a free game. The Trojan can be programmed by the author to perform many actions once activated by the user. These actions usually have malicious intent. The term "Trojan" comes from ancient Greece, where the Greeks used a wooden horse containing hidden Greek soldiers to gain entrance to the city of Troy.

TRUNCATE: The dropping of digits or characters from one end of a data item causing loss of accuracy or information.

TRUTH TABLE: A tabulation of all possible combinations of states at the inputs of a logic gate which will result in a specific logic state at the output of the gate.

TURNKEY SYSTEM: A complete computer system ready to operate without any hardware or software modification or addition.

TWAIN: Stands for Technology Without An Interesting Name.

U

ULTRA-BOOK: An Ultra Book is higher end type of Sub Note Book defined by INTEL.

UNFORMATTED (UNINITIALIZED) DISK: A blank magnetic disk with no track/sector identification recorded on it that allows users to implement their own track/sector identifications.

UNIX: This is an operating system developed by AT&T. It's big push it that it allows one server to service many different end users at one time.

UPLOAD: The process of transferring information from a computer to a web site (or other remote location on a network) and to transfer information from a computer to a web site (or other remote location on a network).

UPS: Universal Power Supply or Uninterruptible Power Supply. An electrical power supply that includes a battery to provide enough power to a computer during an outage to back-up data and properly shut down.

URL: Uniform Resource Locator.
1. The protocol for identifying a document on the Web.
2. A Web address (e.g., www.census.gov).
A URL is unique to each user. See also domain.

USB: Universal Serial Bus. An industry standard for connecting different compatible peripheral devices across multiple platforms. Devices include printers, digital cameras, scanners, game pads, joysticks, keyboards and mice, and storage devices.

USER-FRIENDLY PROGRAM: A software program that has been designed to easily direct the user through the operation or application of a program.
A menu-driven program is considered to be "user-friendly".

USENET: Another name for Internet Newsgroups. A distributed bulletin board system running on news servers, UNIX hosts, on-line services and bulletin board systems. Collectively, all the users who post and read articles to newsgroups. The Usenet is international in scope and is the largest decentralized information utility. The Usenet includes government agencies, universities, high schools, organizations of all sizes as well as millions of stand-alone PCs.

USER: Someone attached to a server or host.

UTILITY: A software program designed to perform a computer system's routine housekeeping functions, like copying, deleting files, and/or providing techniques to simplify the execution of a program.

V

V.42bis: A worldwide modem standard for data compression that lets modems reach data transfer speeds of up to 34,000 bits per second.

VDD: Stands for Virtual Device Driver.

VERONICA: Stands for Very Easy Rodent Oriented Net-wide Index to Computerized Archives. A database of menu names from a large number of Gopher servers. A quick and easy way to search Gopher resources for information by keyword.

VGA: Stands for Video Graphics Adapter. This is a lower level colour monitor.

VIRUS: An unauthorized piece of computer code attached to a computer program or portions of a computer system that secretly copies itself from one computer to another by shared discs and over telephone and cable lines. It can destroy information stored on the computer, and in extreme cases, can destroy operability.

VIDEO TELECONFERENCING: A remote "face-to-face chat," when two or more people using a webcam and an Internet telephone connection chat online. The webcam enables both live voice and video.

VIRTUAL REALITY (VR): A technology that allows one to experience and interact with images in a simulated three-dimensional environment. For example, you could design a room in a house on your computer and actually feel that you are walking around in it even though it was never built. (The Holodeck in the science-fiction TV series *Star Trek*: *Voyager* would be the ultimate virtual reality.) Current technology requires the user to wear a special helmet, viewing goggles, gloves, and other equipment that transmits and receives information from the computer.

VOCABULARY: A list of operating codes or instructions available to the software programmer for writing a program in a specific language.

VOLATILE MEMORY: A memory whose contents are irretrievably lost when power is removed. If data in RAM must be saved after power shut-down, back-up in non-volatile memory (magnetic disk, tape, or CD-R) is essential.

VRML: Stands for Virtual Reality Modeling Language. It's a form of application that gives a 3-D effect to pictures sometimes allowing you to "move" through them.

W

WAIS: Stands for Wide Area Information Servers. Searches large indexes of information on the Internet.

WAIT STATE: An internal condition of delay in processing time executed by the CPU when a synchronizing control signal is not present. Wait states synchronize the timing of a CPU with the relatively slower access time of the computer's main memory.

WAN: Stands for Wide Area Network, like the Internet.

WAV: Stands for WAV form sound format. Microsoft's format for encoding sound files.

WEBCAM: A video camera/computer setup that takes live images and sends them to a Web browser.

WINCHESTER DRIVE: See HARD-DISK DRIVE

WINDOW: A portion of a computer display used in a graphical interface that enables users to select commands by pointing to illustrations or symbols with a mouse. "Windows" is also the name Microsoft adopted for its popular operating system.

WINDOWING: The ability of a program to divide a display screen into smaller sub-units that permit portions of different sections of a program, or different programs, to be displayed on the screen, edited, and copied independently.

WORD PROCESSING (WP): The term refers to a program that allows creating, editing, formatting, displaying, printing, and storage of text with great flexibility and ease. Different WP programs provide different, and sometimes, more desirable capabilities than others.

WORD: The set of binary bits handled by a computer as a primary unit of data. The width (number of bits) of a computer word depends on the hardware design. Wider words imply higher levels of precision, higher speed, and more intricate instructions. Typically, each location in memory contains one word.

WORD PROCESSOR: A computer system or program for setting, editing, revising, correcting, storing, and printing text.

WORLD WIDE WEB ("WWW" OR "THE WEB"): A network of servers on the Internet that use hypertext-linked databases and files. It was developed in 1989 by Tim Berners-Lee, a British computer scientist, and is now the primary platform of the Internet. The feature that distinguishes the Web from other Internet applications is its ability to display graphics in addition to text.

WORM (WRITE-ONCE, READ-MANY): A high-density optical disk memory available in a variety of formats from 5.25" to 14". The WORM can be programmed once, permanently saving a user's data. It then becomes an optical disk read-only memory having essentially the same features as a CD-ROM. Also called CD-R (CD-RECORDABLE).

WORKSTATION: The work area and/or equipment used for computer operations, including computer-aided design (CAD). The equipment generally consists of a monitor, keyboard, printer and/or plotter, and other output devices.

WORKGROUP: Persons sharing files and data between themselves.

WPG: Stands for Word Perfect Graphics.

WRITE: The process of storing data into a memory.

WYSIWYG: What You See Is What You Get. When using most word processors, page layout programs (See desktop publishing), and web page design programs, words and images will be displayed on the monitor as they will look on the printed page or web page.

X-Y-Z

X-Y PLOTTER: A computer-driven printing mechanism that draws coordinate points in graph form.

ZOOM: The process of proportionately enlarging or reducing an image displayed on a computer monitor.

ZIP: Stands for Zone Information Protocol. This is an application that allows for the compression of application files.

www.ingramcontent.com/pod-product-compliance
Lightning Source LLC
LaVergne TN
LVHW092346060326
832902LV00008B/845